AMAZING ANIMALS
SNAKES

BY VALERIE BODDEN

CREATIVE EDUCATION • CREATIVE PAPERBACKS

Published by Creative Education and
Creative Paperbacks
P.O. Box 227, Mankato, Minnesota 56002
Creative Education and Creative Paperbacks are
imprints of The Creative Company
www.thecreativecompany.us

Design by The Design Lab
Production by Angela Korte and Colin O'Dea
Art direction by Rita Marshall
Printed in the United States of America

Photographs by Alamy (BIOSPHOTO), Getty Images
(Tom Bean, DEA PICTURE LIBRARY, dekihendrik/
iStock, George Grall, Hillary Kladke/Moment, Mark
Kostich/E+, David A. Northcott/Corbis Documenta-
ry), iStockphoto (ifish, Mark Kostich), Minden Pictures
(Pete Oxford), Shutterstock (Vince Adam)

Library of Congress Cataloging-in-Publication Data
Names: Bodden, Valerie, author.
Title: Snakes / Valerie Bodden.
Series: Amazing animals.
Includes bibliographical references and index.
Summary: This revised edition surveys key aspects
of snakes, describing the slithering reptiles' appear-
ance, behaviors, and habitats. A folk tale explains
why these creatures do not have legs.
Identifiers: ISBN 978-1-64026-209-6 (hardcover)
/ ISBN 978-1-62832-772-4 (pbk) / ISBN 978-1-
64000-334-7 (eBook)
This title has been submitted for CIP processing under
LCCN 2019937908.

CCSS: RI.1.1, 2, 4, 5, 6, 7; RI.2.2, 5, 6, 7, 10;
RI.3.1, 5, 7, 8; RF.1.1, 3, 4; RF.2.3, 4

First Edition HC 9 8 7 6 5 4 3 2 1
First Edition PBK 9 8 7 6 5 4 3 2 1

Table of Contents

Slithering snakes use their muscles and scales to move.

Snakes are long, thin reptiles.

They do not have legs. There are more than 3,000 kinds of snakes in the world. Many are green or brown. Others are red or black.

reptiles animals that have dry, scaly skin and a body that is always as warm or as cold as the air around it

The forks of a snake's tongue help it locate the source of a scent.

Snakes are covered with scales. These bony plates help protect the reptiles. Snakes have a **forked** tongue. They flick their tongue out to pick up smells from the air.

forked split into two parts

Some snakes are tiny. They can be smaller than a worm. Other snakes are huge. Reticulated pythons can be 25 feet (6.7 m) long! Green anacondas can weigh more than three grown-ups put together!

Snakes continue to grow throughout their lives.

Snakes live everywhere except Antarctica and some islands. Some snakes live in the grass. Others live in forests. Some kinds of snakes live in deserts. Others even live in water.

Sea snakes can stay underwater for two hours at a time.

Snakes

Snakes swallow their meals in one gulp. They can swallow animals bigger than their own heads. Their jaws stretch apart. Some snakes eat frogs or mice. Others eat birds. Big snakes even eat monkeys or deer.

All snakes are carnivores, or meat-eaters.

Most mother snakes lay soft eggs. Baby snakes come out of the eggs. Other mother snakes give birth to babies. Snakes do not take care of their babies. As baby snakes grow, they lose their old skin and grow new skin. As they get older, snakes shed less often.

Baby snakes usually do not eat until they have shed their skin once.

Snakes spend much of the day lying around. If they are cold, they lie in the sun to warm up. If they get too hot, they move to a cooler place.

Snakes like to be alone most of the time.

After a large meal, a snake may not eat for a few months.

Snakes
spend some of their time looking for food. They are silent hunters. When they find **prey**, they strike quickly. Some snakes kill prey by squeezing it. Other snakes have venom. This poisons prey when the snake bites it.

prey animals that are eaten by other animals

Some people keep snakes as pets. Lots of people like to look at snakes in zoos. Others may see snakes outside. It is fun to watch these scaly animals bend and move!

Fewer than 700 kinds of snakes are venomous.

A Snake Tale

People in Africa

used to tell a story about why snakes do not have legs. They said that some animals once had a farm. Someone stole food from the farm. The animals put tar on the ground to trap the thief. It was the snake! The animals pulled the snake out, but his legs stayed stuck in the tar. From then on, the snake had to crawl on his belly!

Read More

Heos, Bridget. *Do You Really Want a Snake?* North Mankato, Minn.: Amicus, 2016.

Kratt, Martin, and Chris Kratt. *Wild Reptiles: Snakes, Crocodiles, Lizards, and Turtles!* New York: Random House, 2015.

Turnbull, Stephanie. *Snake*. Mankato, Minn.: Smart Apple Media, 2015.

Websites

Enchanted Learning: Snakes
http://www.enchantedlearning.com/painting/snakes.shtml
This site has lots of snake coloring pages.

Idaho Public Television: Science Trek: Snakes
http://idahoptv.org/sciencetrek/topics/snakes/index.cfm
Watch a video and read more about snakes!

San Diego Zoo Kids: Anaconda
https://kids.sandiegozoo.org/animals/anaconda
Learn about the different kinds of anacondas.

Index